50 Classic Cocktails: Mixology Made Simple Recipes

By: Kelly Johnson

Table of Contents

- Martini
- Margarita
- Old Fashioned
- Mojito
- Negroni
- Manhattan
- Daiquiri
- Whiskey Sour
- Moscow Mule
- Piña Colada
- Cosmopolitan
- Mai Tai
- Bloody Mary
- Tom Collins
- Long Island Iced Tea
- Gin and Tonic
- Tequila Sunrise
- Sazerac
- Caipirinha
- French 75
- Aperol Spritz
- Paloma
- Rum Punch
- Mint Julep
- Vesper Martini
- Pimm's Cup
- Sidecar
- Rob Roy
- Amaretto Sour
- Gimlet
- Brandy Alexander
- Hurricane
- Cuba Libre
- Tom Collins
- Black Russian

- White Russian
- Mai Tai
- Manhattan
- Bellini
- Clover Club
- Blackberry Bramble
- Peach Fizz
- Gold Rush
- Ramos Gin Fizz
- Blue Lagoon
- Cherry Bounce
- Espresso Martini
- Pisco Sour
- Basil Smash
- Tequila Sour

Martini

Ingredients:

- 2 1/2 oz gin (or vodka for a vodka martini)
- 1/2 oz dry vermouth
- Lemon twist or olive for garnish

Instructions:

1. Fill a mixing glass with ice and pour in the gin and vermouth.
2. Stir well for about 30 seconds until chilled.
3. Strain into a chilled martini glass.
4. Garnish with a lemon twist or an olive.

Margarita

Ingredients:

- 2 oz tequila
- 1 oz lime juice (freshly squeezed)
- 1 oz triple sec (or Cointreau)
- Salt for rimming the glass (optional)
- Lime wedge for garnish

Instructions:

1. Rim the glass with lime juice and dip it into salt if desired.
2. Fill a shaker with ice and add tequila, lime juice, and triple sec.
3. Shake well until chilled, then strain into the prepared glass.
4. Garnish with a lime wedge.

Old Fashioned

Ingredients:

- 2 oz bourbon or rye whiskey
- 1 sugar cube
- 2 dashes Angostura bitters
- Orange peel for garnish

Instructions:

1. Place the sugar cube in an old fashioned glass and add bitters.
2. Muddle the sugar and bitters together.
3. Add a large ice cube, then pour the whiskey over it.
4. Stir gently to combine and garnish with a twist of orange peel.

Mojito

Ingredients:

- 2 oz white rum
- 1 oz lime juice (freshly squeezed)
- 2 tsp sugar (or simple syrup)
- 6-8 fresh mint leaves
- Soda water
- Lime wedge and mint sprig for garnish

Instructions:

1. Muddle the mint leaves and sugar in a glass.
2. Add lime juice and rum, then fill the glass with ice.
3. Top with soda water and stir gently.
4. Garnish with a lime wedge and mint sprig.

Negroni

Ingredients:

- 1 oz gin
- 1 oz Campari
- 1 oz sweet vermouth
- Orange peel for garnish

Instructions:

1. Fill a mixing glass with ice and add gin, Campari, and vermouth.
2. Stir until well-chilled and strain into a rocks glass filled with ice.
3. Garnish with an orange peel.

Manhattan

Ingredients:

- 2 oz bourbon or rye whiskey
- 1 oz sweet vermouth
- 2 dashes Angostura bitters
- Maraschino cherry for garnish

Instructions:

1. Fill a mixing glass with ice and add whiskey, vermouth, and bitters.
2. Stir until chilled, then strain into a chilled coupe glass.
3. Garnish with a maraschino cherry.

Daiquiri

Ingredients:

- 2 oz white rum
- 1 oz lime juice (freshly squeezed)
- 3/4 oz simple syrup

Instructions:

1. Fill a shaker with ice and add rum, lime juice, and simple syrup.
2. Shake well until chilled, then strain into a chilled coupe glass.
3. Garnish with a lime wheel.

Whiskey Sour

Ingredients:

- 2 oz bourbon
- 3/4 oz fresh lemon juice
- 1/2 oz simple syrup
- Lemon slice and cherry for garnish

Instructions:

1. Fill a shaker with ice and add bourbon, lemon juice, and simple syrup.
2. Shake well until chilled, then strain into a rocks glass with ice.
3. Garnish with a lemon slice and cherry.

Moscow Mule

Ingredients:

- 2 oz vodka
- 1 oz lime juice (freshly squeezed)
- 4 oz ginger beer
- Lime wedge and mint sprig for garnish

Instructions:

1. Fill a copper mug with ice.
2. Add vodka and lime juice.
3. Top with ginger beer and stir gently.
4. Garnish with a lime wedge and mint sprig.

Piña Colada

Ingredients:

- 2 oz white rum
- 1 oz coconut cream
- 3 oz pineapple juice
- Pineapple wedge and maraschino cherry for garnish

Instructions:

1. Fill a blender with ice and add rum, coconut cream, and pineapple juice.
2. Blend until smooth.
3. Pour into a chilled glass and garnish with a pineapple wedge and cherry.

Cosmopolitan

Ingredients:

- 1 1/2 oz vodka
- 1 oz cranberry juice
- 1/2 oz triple sec (or Cointreau)
- 1/2 oz lime juice (freshly squeezed)
- Lime wheel or twist for garnish

Instructions:

1. Fill a shaker with ice and add vodka, cranberry juice, triple sec, and lime juice.
2. Shake well until chilled, then strain into a chilled coupe glass.
3. Garnish with a lime wheel or twist.

Mai Tai

Ingredients:

- 1 oz light rum
- 1 oz dark rum
- 1/2 oz lime juice (freshly squeezed)
- 1/2 oz orange liqueur (like Curaçao)
- 1/2 oz orgeat syrup
- Mint sprig and lime wheel for garnish

Instructions:

1. Fill a shaker with ice and add light rum, dark rum, lime juice, orange liqueur, and orgeat syrup.
2. Shake until well-chilled, then strain into a glass filled with crushed ice.
3. Garnish with a mint sprig and lime wheel.

Bloody Mary

Ingredients:

- 2 oz vodka
- 4 oz tomato juice
- 1/2 oz lemon juice (freshly squeezed)
- 2 dashes Worcestershire sauce
- 2 dashes hot sauce (like Tabasco)
- Pinch of salt and pepper
- Celery stick, pickle, or olives for garnish

Instructions:

1. Fill a shaker with ice and add vodka, tomato juice, lemon juice, Worcestershire sauce, hot sauce, salt, and pepper.
2. Shake gently to combine, then strain into a tall glass filled with ice.
3. Garnish with a celery stick, pickle, or olives.

Tom Collins

Ingredients:

- 2 oz gin
- 1 oz lemon juice (freshly squeezed)
- 1/2 oz simple syrup
- 4 oz soda water
- Lemon slice and cherry for garnish

Instructions:

1. Fill a shaker with ice and add gin, lemon juice, and simple syrup.
2. Shake well and strain into a tall glass filled with ice.
3. Top with soda water and garnish with a lemon slice and cherry.

Long Island Iced Tea

Ingredients:

- 1/2 oz vodka
- 1/2 oz rum
- 1/2 oz gin
- 1/2 oz tequila
- 1/2 oz triple sec
- 1 oz lemon juice (freshly squeezed)
- 1 oz simple syrup
- Splash of cola
- Lemon wedge for garnish

Instructions:

1. Fill a shaker with ice and add vodka, rum, gin, tequila, triple sec, lemon juice, and simple syrup.
2. Shake well and strain into a tall glass filled with ice.
3. Top with a splash of cola and garnish with a lemon wedge.

Gin and Tonic

Ingredients:

- 2 oz gin
- 4 oz tonic water
- Lime wedge for garnish

Instructions:

1. Fill a glass with ice.
2. Add gin and top with tonic water.
3. Stir gently and garnish with a lime wedge.

Tequila Sunrise

Ingredients:

- 2 oz tequila
- 4 oz orange juice
- 1/2 oz grenadine
- Orange slice and cherry for garnish

Instructions:

1. Fill a highball glass with ice.
2. Pour tequila and orange juice into the glass and stir.
3. Slowly pour grenadine into the glass. It will settle at the bottom, creating a sunrise effect.
4. Garnish with an orange slice and cherry.

Sazerac

Ingredients:

- 2 oz rye whiskey
- 1 sugar cube
- 2 dashes Peychaud's bitters
- 1 dash Angostura bitters
- Absinthe (or absinthe substitute)
- Lemon peel for garnish

Instructions:

1. Muddle the sugar and bitters in a glass.
2. Add rye whiskey and stir until the sugar dissolves.
3. Rinse another glass with a small amount of absinthe, discard the excess, and pour the whiskey mixture into it.
4. Garnish with a lemon peel.

Caipirinha

Ingredients:

- 2 oz cachaça
- 1 lime, cut into wedges
- 2 tsp sugar

Instructions:

1. Muddle the lime wedges and sugar together in a glass.
2. Fill the glass with ice, add cachaça, and stir.
3. Serve with a lime wedge garnish.

French 75

Ingredients:

- 1 oz gin
- 1/2 oz lemon juice (freshly squeezed)
- 1/2 oz simple syrup
- 3 oz Champagne or sparkling wine
- Lemon twist for garnish

Instructions:

1. Shake gin, lemon juice, and simple syrup with ice.
2. Strain into a Champagne flute.
3. Top with Champagne and garnish with a lemon twist.

Aperol Spritz

Ingredients:

- 3 oz Aperol
- 2 oz Prosecco
- 1 oz soda water
- Orange slice for garnish

Instructions:

1. Fill a glass with ice and add Aperol.
2. Pour in Prosecco and top with soda water.
3. Stir gently and garnish with an orange slice.

Paloma

Ingredients:

- 2 oz tequila
- 1/2 oz lime juice (freshly squeezed)
- 4 oz grapefruit soda (or freshly squeezed grapefruit juice and soda water)
- Pinch of salt
- Lime wedge and salt for rimming the glass

Instructions:

1. Rim a glass with salt and fill with ice.
2. Add tequila, lime juice, and grapefruit soda to the glass.
3. Stir gently and garnish with a lime wedge.

Rum Punch

Ingredients:

- 2 oz rum (light or dark)
- 1 oz orange juice
- 1 oz pineapple juice
- 1/2 oz grenadine
- 1/4 oz lime juice
- Pineapple slice and cherry for garnish

Instructions:

1. Fill a shaker with ice and add rum, juices, and grenadine.
2. Shake well and strain into a tall glass filled with ice.
3. Garnish with a pineapple slice and cherry.

Mint Julep

Ingredients:

- 2 oz bourbon
- 1/2 oz simple syrup
- 8-10 fresh mint leaves
- Crushed ice
- Mint sprig for garnish

Instructions:

1. Muddle mint leaves and simple syrup in a glass.
2. Fill the glass with crushed ice and add bourbon.
3. Stir gently and garnish with a mint sprig.

Vesper Martini

Ingredients:

- 3 oz vodka
- 1 oz gin
- 1/2 oz Lillet Blanc
- Lemon twist for garnish

Instructions:

1. Fill a mixing glass with ice.
2. Add vodka, gin, and Lillet Blanc.
3. Stir until well-chilled.
4. Strain into a chilled cocktail glass.
5. Garnish with a lemon twist.

Pimm's Cup

Ingredients:

- 2 oz Pimm's No. 1
- 4 oz lemonade
- 1 oz soda water
- Cucumber slices, orange slices, and strawberry halves for garnish

Instructions:

1. Fill a highball glass with ice.
2. Add Pimm's, lemonade, and soda water.
3. Stir gently to combine.
4. Garnish with cucumber slices, orange slices, and strawberry halves.

Sidecar

Ingredients:

- 2 oz cognac
- 1 oz Cointreau
- 3/4 oz lemon juice (freshly squeezed)
- Sugar for rimming the glass
- Lemon twist for garnish

Instructions:

1. Rim the edge of a cocktail glass with sugar.
2. Fill a shaker with ice and add cognac, Cointreau, and lemon juice.
3. Shake well until well-chilled.
4. Strain into the prepared glass.
5. Garnish with a lemon twist.

Rob Roy

Ingredients:

- 2 oz Scotch whisky
- 1 oz sweet vermouth
- 2 dashes Angostura bitters
- Maraschino cherry for garnish

Instructions:

1. Fill a mixing glass with ice.
2. Add Scotch whisky, sweet vermouth, and bitters.
3. Stir until well-chilled.
4. Strain into a chilled cocktail glass.
5. Garnish with a maraschino cherry.

Amaretto Sour

Ingredients:

- 2 oz amaretto
- 3/4 oz lemon juice (freshly squeezed)
- 1/2 oz simple syrup
- Lemon twist and maraschino cherry for garnish

Instructions:

1. Fill a shaker with ice.
2. Add amaretto, lemon juice, and simple syrup.
3. Shake well until chilled.
4. Strain into an old-fashioned glass filled with ice.
5. Garnish with a lemon twist and maraschino cherry.

Gimlet

Ingredients:

- 2 oz gin
- 1 oz lime juice (freshly squeezed)
- 1/2 oz simple syrup
- Lime wheel for garnish

Instructions:

1. Fill a shaker with ice.
2. Add gin, lime juice, and simple syrup.
3. Shake well until well-chilled.
4. Strain into a chilled cocktail glass.
5. Garnish with a lime wheel.

Brandy Alexander

Ingredients:

- 1 oz brandy
- 1 oz dark crème de cacao
- 2 oz heavy cream
- Nutmeg for garnish

Instructions:

1. Fill a shaker with ice.
2. Add brandy, dark crème de cacao, and heavy cream.
3. Shake well until well-chilled.
4. Strain into a chilled cocktail glass.
5. Garnish with freshly grated nutmeg.

Hurricane

Ingredients:

- 2 oz light rum
- 2 oz dark rum
- 1 oz passion fruit juice
- 1 oz orange juice
- 1/2 oz grenadine
- Pineapple wedge and cherry for garnish

Instructions:

1. Fill a shaker with ice and add both rums, passion fruit juice, orange juice, and grenadine.
2. Shake well until well-chilled.
3. Strain into a hurricane glass filled with ice.
4. Garnish with a pineapple wedge and cherry.

Cuba Libre

Ingredients:

- 2 oz rum (light)
- 4 oz cola
- 1/2 oz lime juice (freshly squeezed)
- Lime wedge for garnish

Instructions:

1. Fill a highball glass with ice.
2. Add rum and lime juice.
3. Top with cola and stir gently.
4. Garnish with a lime wedge.

Tom Collins

Ingredients:

- 2 oz gin
- 1 oz lemon juice (freshly squeezed)
- 1/2 oz simple syrup
- 2 oz soda water
- Lemon wheel and cherry for garnish

Instructions:

1. Fill a shaker with ice and add gin, lemon juice, and simple syrup.
2. Shake well and strain into a tall glass filled with ice.
3. Top with soda water and stir gently.
4. Garnish with a lemon wheel and cherry.

Black Russian

Ingredients:

- 2 oz vodka
- 1 oz coffee liqueur (such as Kahlúa)

Instructions:

1. Fill a glass with ice.
2. Pour vodka and coffee liqueur into the glass.
3. Stir gently and serve.

White Russian

Ingredients:

- 2 oz vodka
- 1 oz coffee liqueur
- 1 oz heavy cream

Instructions:

1. Fill a glass with ice.
2. Pour vodka and coffee liqueur into the glass.
3. Top with heavy cream and stir gently.
4. Serve.

Mai Tai

Ingredients:

- 1 oz light rum
- 1 oz dark rum
- 1/2 oz lime juice (freshly squeezed)
- 1/2 oz orange curaçao
- 1/2 oz orgeat syrup
- Lime wheel and mint sprig for garnish

Instructions:

1. Fill a shaker with ice and add light rum, lime juice, orange curaçao, and orgeat syrup.
2. Shake well and strain into a rocks glass filled with ice.
3. Float dark rum on top by pouring it gently over the back of a spoon.
4. Garnish with a lime wheel and mint sprig.

Manhattan

Ingredients:

- 2 oz rye whiskey (or bourbon)
- 1 oz sweet vermouth
- 2 dashes Angostura bitters
- Cherry for garnish

Instructions:

1. Fill a mixing glass with ice.
2. Add rye whiskey, sweet vermouth, and bitters.
3. Stir until well-chilled.
4. Strain into a chilled cocktail glass.
5. Garnish with a cherry.

Bellini

Ingredients:

- 2 oz peach purée
- 4 oz Prosecco (or Champagne)

Instructions:

1. Pour peach purée into a flute glass.
2. Slowly top with chilled Prosecco.
3. Stir gently to combine.
4. Serve immediately.

Clover Club

Ingredients:

- 2 oz gin
- 1 oz lemon juice (freshly squeezed)
- 1/2 oz raspberry syrup (or raspberry liqueur)
- 1 egg white (optional for froth)
- Fresh raspberries for garnish

Instructions:

1. Fill a shaker with ice and add gin, lemon juice, raspberry syrup, and egg white (if using).
2. Shake vigorously to create froth.
3. Strain into a chilled coupe glass.
4. Garnish with fresh raspberries.

Blackberry Bramble

Ingredients:

- 2 oz gin
- 1 oz blackberry liqueur (such as Crème de Mure)
- 1 oz lemon juice (freshly squeezed)
- 1/2 oz simple syrup
- Blackberries for garnish

Instructions:

1. Fill a shaker with ice and add gin, blackberry liqueur, lemon juice, and simple syrup.
2. Shake well and strain into a glass filled with crushed ice.
3. Garnish with fresh blackberries.

Peach Fizz

Ingredients:

- 2 oz peach purée
- 1 oz lemon juice (freshly squeezed)
- 1 oz simple syrup
- 2 oz soda water
- Peach slice for garnish

Instructions:

1. Fill a shaker with ice and add peach purée, lemon juice, and simple syrup.
2. Shake well and strain into a highball glass filled with ice.
3. Top with soda water and stir gently.
4. Garnish with a peach slice.

Gold Rush

Ingredients:

- 2 oz bourbon
- 3/4 oz honey syrup (mix equal parts honey and water)
- 3/4 oz lemon juice (freshly squeezed)

Instructions:

1. Fill a shaker with ice and add bourbon, honey syrup, and lemon juice.
2. Shake well until chilled.
3. Strain into a rocks glass filled with ice.
4. Serve.

Ramos Gin Fizz

Ingredients:

- 2 oz gin
- 1 oz heavy cream
- 1 oz lemon juice (freshly squeezed)
- 1 oz lime juice (freshly squeezed)
- 1/2 oz simple syrup
- 2 dashes orange flower water
- 1 egg white (optional for froth)
- Soda water

Instructions:

1. Fill a shaker with ice and add gin, cream, lemon juice, lime juice, simple syrup, orange flower water, and egg white (if using).
2. Shake vigorously for 10-15 seconds to create froth.
3. Strain into a tall glass without ice.
4. Top with soda water and serve.

Blue Lagoon

Ingredients:

- 1 1/2 oz vodka
- 1 oz blue curaçao
- 1 oz lemonade
- Lemon slice for garnish

Instructions:

1. Fill a shaker with ice and add vodka, blue curaçao, and lemonade.
2. Shake well and strain into a glass filled with ice.
3. Garnish with a lemon slice.

Cherry Bounce

Ingredients:

- 2 oz bourbon
- 1 oz cherry liqueur (such as Luxardo)
- 1/2 oz simple syrup
- 2 dashes Angostura bitters
- Maraschino cherry for garnish

Instructions:

1. Fill a mixing glass with ice and add bourbon, cherry liqueur, simple syrup, and bitters.
2. Stir until well-chilled.
3. Strain into a rocks glass filled with ice.
4. Garnish with a maraschino cherry.

Espresso Martini

Ingredients:

- 2 oz vodka
- 1 oz coffee liqueur (such as Kahlúa)
- 1 oz freshly brewed espresso
- Coffee beans for garnish

Instructions:

1. Fill a shaker with ice and add vodka, coffee liqueur, and espresso.
2. Shake vigorously until well-chilled.
3. Strain into a chilled martini glass.
4. Garnish with coffee beans.

Pisco Sour

Ingredients:

- 2 oz pisco
- 1 oz lemon juice (freshly squeezed)
- 3/4 oz simple syrup
- 1 egg white (optional for froth)
- Angostura bitters for garnish

Instructions:

1. Fill a shaker with ice and add pisco, lemon juice, simple syrup, and egg white (if using).
2. Shake vigorously to create froth.
3. Strain into a chilled glass.
4. Add a few dashes of Angostura bitters on top.

Basil Smash

Ingredients:

- 2 oz gin
- 3-4 fresh basil leaves
- 3/4 oz lemon juice (freshly squeezed)
- 1/2 oz simple syrup

Instructions:

1. Muddle basil leaves in a shaker.
2. Add gin, lemon juice, and simple syrup.
3. Fill the shaker with ice and shake well.
4. Strain into a rocks glass filled with ice.
5. Garnish with a basil leaf.

Tequila Sour

Ingredients:

- 2 oz tequila (blanco or reposado)
- 1 oz lemon juice (freshly squeezed)
- 3/4 oz simple syrup
- Egg white (optional for froth)
- Lemon twist for garnish

Instructions:

1. Fill a shaker with ice and add tequila, lemon juice, simple syrup, and egg white (if using).
2. Shake vigorously until well-chilled.
3. Strain into a chilled glass.
4. Garnish with a lemon twist.

www.ingramcontent.com/pod-product-compliance
Lightning Source LLC
LaVergne TN
LVHW081333060526
838201LV00055B/2622